# Love in the Time of Covid

### poems

### from 2020

## by David Laing Dawson

copyright @ 2020 David Laing Dawson

All rights reserved

**ISBN:** 9798682193998

For

Dean

Lauryn

Jordyn

Jacqueline

Sophie

Avery

Taryn

Matthew

(the grandchildren, so far)

**It is in isolation that**

**The self**

**Discovers how much**

**It is defined by others**

I watch the buds on our maple turn from a deep brown with a hint of red into a lighter brown, a sepia centre with a fringe of ochre. It is a long cold spring and day after day the fringe of ochre grows perceptibly but the green doesn't come.

And I wonder for a moment if the green might never come in this year of the virus. It is the way I can imagine the end of days, as the failure of Spring.

But then I realize it is the first time I ever so closely watched this transition to life renewed. And I know the green will come, first in the lightest of shades, a grey sage, and then an olive yellow, and finally, for one more season at least, a deep absorbing viridian.

## COVID Dreams

A restlessness abounds
And finds a venue in sleep
Dancing from problem to problem
Around the world and back.
Faces merge, proclaim, obstruct
And old sins of shame
Join the quest for survival.

The tall engineer tells us all
That the small river below
Contains sufficient genetic diversity
To handle all the human waste
We pour into it.
To make his point he dives
And somehow bounces
And then stands before us
Covered in shit.
I try to point this out
But my voice is feeble
And they are not listening.

**It is in the embrace of routine**

**We find peace**

**And in its escape**

**That we find life.**

It is quiet now
And when it is quiet
I am too alone with my thoughts.

I take up a brush to paint
For the act of painting
Creates obstacle and struggle,
Failure, disappointment,
The fleeting pleasure
Of creation.

Christo died at the end of May.
He wrapped things.

**My dreams grow long and strange**

**Bending time and place.**

**In the day the hot and humid air**

**Gives way to dancing leaves.**

**I look for omens**

**And find none.**

## Jervis Bay Dunes

Beyond the sand there is sky
And you know this sky
Lies above water
And shares its mists
Its reflections
And dreams.

## Horizon

Above the field there is a blue
Like no other,
And clouds that come alive
Where the thin horizon beckons.
It is a line some day
We all must cross.

## Horizon II

For a century artists have fought
With the horizon.
Some called it a tyranny,
That disappearing focal point
The edge of our sight.
That fixed line
Determining all other lines.
Some have ignored it
Or turned it on end
Or broken it apart.
Some have relinquished the illusion of depth
And let the wall behind the canvas
Be the limit of our perception.
Yet it remains, the horizon,
In both visual reality
And metaphorical adventure:
Anxiety, mystery, discovery,
Sunset, sunrise, birth and death.
It is still there.
Why not embrace it?

It is not an easy thing
To live within the narrative
Of love and hope and
If not happy endings then
At least, at least,
Fulfillment
However transient
Ephemeral
Distant
Delusional.
But, but there is
A child's smile.
That is something.

## **On the Trent**

I sit in the moment
When the breeze from river to shore
Slows and stops, and the smoke
From my fire rises upward.
The sun is low in the trees
And splatters the leaves with white gold
The skies darken
The lands cool
The river beckons the breeze
And the smoke
From my waning fire.
And I, if it is still reasonable to think of an I,
Retire to my bed.

Some fat black ants have made their way
Into our kitchen.
They seem to be free spirits
Roaming carelessly,
Seeking particles of food.
I have a Buddhist impulse to let them be,
Courtesy, I think, of our new found friend,
Covid Nineteen.

The eyes see

And the heart interprets

(all right, I know it's the brain,

but just this once let me be a poet)

And all the eyes see is reflection,

Light that is not absorbed.

So be it water or sky

Or something in between

We must manufacture

Our own reality

From scant information,

And then decide if we want to

Linger here a while longer.

The winds came softly at first
Then in gusts with quiet between
A quiet that could bring another gust
Or
Perhaps nothing would follow
But then another gust would come
And quiet would follow.
The doctors call it Cheyne-Stokes
A breathing pattern that precedes
Death
A time of no wind at all.

To sit in morning silence
As the leaves unfold
And watch the smallest movement
With fair trade coffee in hand
- Now that is enlightenment.

The days and weeks slip by,
The news is not good.
I track the virus as it
Moves and flourishes
Here and there,
Cutting a swath through human
Hubris and greed.
In my dreams I revisit
My mistakes and failures
As if called upon to do so
At the end of times.
And yet there is another side to this
That makes itself apparent
In the quiet of our solitude,
In the movement of the clouds,
In the being here this moment,
But maybe not the next.

Where but the sky
Should dreams take us
When reality is hard to bear
When a thing too small to see
Threatens our fragile hold
On the fiction of
Permanence.

With humans quiet
The birds glide with ease
Above the pool
Beneath the branches.
They swoop into tunnels
Between the leaves
While others circle beyond the trees
Or pass in threes and fours.
They seem to show less fear
Less hesitation.
But have they changed
Or have I?

The sky, ahh the sky.
On the prairies
To see it all
I must turn and bend

And I see that here
It is not just back drop
Not merely a small canopy
Above a tree or hill

Not merely air and cloud,
Refracted light
The weightless above
The heavy earth.

Here the sky is
Not even an equal partner
In this landscape
But a greater infinite thing

Of astonishing depth
And weight and movement
Of shifting forms and colours
That stretch - yes on the prairies

You can see it - that stretch
That stretch beyond my imagination
And hold this spinning orb
In sometimes gentle hands.

Fields of sorghum and wheat
Flowing from ochre to yellow green
And then deep viridian
In the grasses
Surrounding still ponds
Alive with growth
And abundance.
Take your hand,
Reach out
And brush it softly;
Imagined hand caressing
This living earth.

A wall of conifers
Foretells the mystery beyond,
The slanting fractured rays
Of sunlight darkening.



In the Strait beyond Sooke
The fog awaits its turn
To creep into the inlets and basins,
Bringing with it the chill of eternity.



A palm alone is plaintive
Bending in the off shore winds
Rooted in the grasslands
That are soon to be submerged.

There is a moment in our Cootes
When the willows yellow
And the vines redden
While the others stay with winter.


During this hour the breezes settle
Flowing neither to nor from the lake
It is a brief moment of stillness,
And of prayer.

# Also by David Laing Dawson

**Plays**

- Whose Mind is it Anyway?
- The Waiting Room
- My Name is Walter James Cross
- Here, Not There
- Modern Times, almost a Musical
- Assisted Living
- The Decision
- MacBush, the Musical
- If There is a River

**Films**

- Walter
- Who Cares
- Manic
- Cutting for Stone
- Painting with Tom, David, and Emily
- Stray Dogs
- Schizophrenia in Focus
- The Brush, the Pen, and Recovery

**Novels**
- Last Rights
- Double Blind
- Essondale
- The Intern
- Slide in all Direction
- Don't Look Down

**Short Story Collection**

- The Butterscotch Palace

**Poetry/paintings**
- A Feathered Symmetry
- Painting is silent poetry, and Poetry is painting with words.

**Non Fiction**

- Schizophrenia in Focus
- The Borderline Patient, relationship management
- The Adolescent Owner's Manual
- Two years of Trump on the Psychiatrists Couch
- Mind You

Made in the USA
Columbia, SC
21 September 2020